THE LITTLE BOOK OF
TEQUILA

Published by OH!
20 Mortimer Street
London W1T 3JW

Text © 2021 OH!
Design © 2021 OH!

ISBN 978-1-80069-027-1

Compiled by: Malcolm Croft
Editorial: Victoria Godden, Lisa Dyer
Project manager: Russell Porter
Design: Tony Seddon
Production: Freencky Portas

A CIP catalogue record for this book is available from the British Library

Printed in Dubai

10 9 8 7 6 5 4 3 2 1

Illustrations: Freepik.com

THE LITTLE BOOK OF

TEQUILA

SHOT TO PERFECTION

CONTENTS

INTRODUCTION

Damas y caballeros, welcome to this tiny tome about the coolest rising star in all of the spirit world – tequila!

Now, when it comes to winning at twenty-first-century booze consumption, this one-of-a-kind Mexican honey water, lovingly extracted from just a single species of the agave plant, calls all the shots. However, while tequila may now be the most on-trend spirit in the world, it still remains the most misunderstood. Once upon a time – let's say the entire twentieth century – tequila's worldwide reputation (except in Mexico) hovered above the gutter; it was the sole spirit that, as one quipster once wisecracked, "made those who ingested it want to both fight *and* f**k" (often at the same time). Not even nasty vodka is that cruel. Tequila, particularly in the United States (where it was the nation's first natively produced alcohol, remember), was the loud host of any party you didn't really want to be seen at, a weapon of mass intoxication that would fire back if shot first, and the drink most responsible for dehydrated souls to utter those immortal words, "I'm never drinking again."

Well, those days are long gone. And, I mean, vanished. Today, tequila is as classy as any booze can be allowed to become. Tequila shots are as passé as the frat/college culture that cultivated them. Civilized millennials and Gen Z'ers, the world's largest consumer group, wouldn't be seen dead with a *mixto* – the only type of tequila the world gave a shit about until premium Patrón came along.

Modern hyper-super-ultra-mega sipping tequila is, well, George Clooney in a glass. Helen Mirren in a highball. It is the height of sophistication. No shirt-and-shoes dinner party is worth its salt without it. Of course, it's always been that way in Mexico; the rest of the world is only now just catching up to the *real* tequila, the drink that will knock your socks off, but only because of how smooth, deep and rich it is, not because of how bad you feel the next morning. As Dwayne Johnson has no doubt probably posted to his 'gram, if you get a hangover drinking tequila, you ain't doing it right.

So, truth, statistics and salvation lies within this little book of tequila-infused fun. Pass on what you know, and share your love of only good tequila – 100 per cent agave – and forget the rest. You're welcome.

Salud!

CHAPTER
ONE

THE GOLD RUSH

The Legend of Tequila

There are many myths surrounding tequila, but none more so amazing that its origin story. The Aztecs, known for their agricultural nous, and who settled in Mexico in the thirteenth to the fifteenth centuries, supposedly discovered tequila... by divine intervention?

One day, so the story goes, a lightning strike struck an agave plant on top of tequila's conical, mythical volcano, causing the plant to ooze its famously sweet and intoxicating elixir of the Gods. The Aztecs turned it into a boozy milkshake, *pulque*.

Good Gods

The Olmecs, a Mexican civilization even more ancient than the ancient Aztecs, and dating back before 1000 BC, worshipped the milky goodness which sprung from the maguey (agave) plant so much that they toasted two gods in its honour.

The first was Mayahuel, the goddess of the agave plant, and the second was Patecatl, the god of *pulque*.

Tequila Cocktail:

LONG ISLAND ICED TEA

Without doubt the booziest cocktail ever devised, the Long Island Iced Tea will have you singing The Champs' "Tequila" in no time. Of course, you can leave out the vodka, gin, triple sec and rum if you like, and just have a large Charro Negro – but variety is the spice of this particular cocktail.

Mix and Match:

1½ oz vanilla vodka
1½ oz London dry gin
1½ oz reposado tequila
1½ oz rum
1½ oz triple sec

1½ oz fresh lime juice
Half a jug of ice cubes
Cola (fill to the top)
2 limes, cut into wedges

Make It Right:

- Pour the spirits into a large jug, and add the lime juice.

- Half-fill the jug with large ice cubes, then stir until the jug feels cold on the outside.

- Add the cola and stir.

- Drop in the lime wedges.

- Drink from the jug. Or, if civilized, divide into highball glasses.

NOM *(Norma Oficial Mexicana)*

Next time you have a tequila (now?), inspect the bottle's label. The acronym NOM, or Norma Oficial Mexicana, is important. The four-digit NOM designation refers to the distillery code where the tequila was made. All tequila bottles carry a NOM.

There are 135 active tequila distilleries in Mexico, but only eight distilleries are dedicated to producing a single brand.

1108: *Tequileño*

1114: *El Caballito Cerrero*

1120: *Siete Leguas*

1127: *Chinaco*

1451: *Sierra*

1492: *Patrón*

1493: *Fortaleza*

1530: *Suerte*

In the Limelight:

PATRÓN *NOM: 1492*

Produced at Hacienda Patrón on the edge of Atotonilco El Alto, Patrón is the only brand to be designated the NOM 1492, and was undoubtedly the first premium tequila exported to the US, in the late 1980s. The brand prides itself on using blue agave plants with a higher sugar content than the average *piña* (or heart of the agave plant). While the standard *piña* has 22 per cent sugar, Patrón proudly boasts 26 per cent. The brand also claim that "more than 60 hands will inspect every single bottle before it is shipped."

In 2018, Patrón was sold to Bacardi, the world's largest privately held spirits company, for $5.1 billion – the largest single drinks company sale ever!

Tequila Cocktails:
THE BANDERA

Liven up your next house party with
a traditional Mexican specialty – the
Bandera, or Flag.

- Fill up three shots glasses that
  represent the three colours of the
  Mexican flag – red, white, and green
  – and neck each one in that order.
- Red – Sangrita (a traditional tequila
  chaser)
- White – neat blanco tequila
- Green – lime juice chaser

Know Thy Tequila

Here is an old Mexican folk saying:

Para el cruel destino, vino;
Para el fracaso, de tequila un vaso;
Para la tristeza, cerveza;
Para todo mal, mezcal.

For cruel fate, wine;
For failure, a glass of tequila;
For sadness, beer;
For everything bad, mezcal.

Tequila Brands Owned by Celebrities

Tequila has become the hottest must-own spirit of celebrities in recent years, finally surpassing vodka, gin and whisky as the go-to tax haven of choice. Just kidding.

1. **Dwayne Johnson** – *Teremana*
2. **Rita Ora** – *Próspero*
3. **Adam Levine and Sammy Hagar** – *Santo Mezquila*
4. **AC/DC** – *Thunderstruck Tequila*
5. **George Clooney and Rande Gerber** – *Casamigos*
6. **Toby Keith** – *Wild Shot Mezcal*
7. **Justin Timberlake** – *Sauza 901*
8. **P Diddy (Sean Combs)** – *DeLeón*
9. **Carlos Santana** – *Casa Noble*
10. **Bryan Cranston and Aaron Paul** – *Dos Hombres*

A Little Horse, Part 1

A traditional tequila glass is called a *caballito* ("little horse" in Spanish) or a *tequillita*. Which is apt, considering too much tequila can make your voice a little hoarse.

Anyway, this 2-ounce glass is 3½ inches tall and has a flat bottom and a wide mouth. The traditional Mexican version is typically taller and thinner than the US and UK counterparts.

Tequila Days of the Year

Let's clear up the confusion and get these tequila toastin' dates straight:

- **National Tequila Day (US)**: 24 July (see page 111)
- **National Tequila Day (Mexico)**: the third Saturday in March
- **Mexican Independence Day**: 16 September (It commemorates the day in 1810 when Mexicans revolted against Spain's colonial rule.)
- **Día de los Muertos (Day of the Dead)**: 31 October to 2 November (A glass of tequila is placed on graves as a sign of respect for the dead)
- **Cinco de Mayo**: 5 May (Created by Corona beer's marketing team as a way to drink more beer – not celebrated by Mexicans at all)
- **National Margarita Day (US)**: 22 February (Because why not?)

In the Limelight:

SAUZA *NOM: 1102*

Founded in 1873, the Casa Sauza distillery at La Perseverancia sprang to life when then-17-year-old Don Cenobio Sauza – the "father of tequila" – distilled all he learnt from his internship at the Cuervo family to start his own tequila brand.

Legend tells us that it was Sauza who crossed over the El Paso del Norte border with three casks and six jugs of his tequila to became the first exporter of tequila into the US – the world's largest tequila consumer. He also shortened the name from "tequila extract" to "tequila". It's cleaner.

Feeling Blue

Agave tequilana weber is the Latin classification name for tequila's main natural ingredient – the blue agave plant. These lily-like succulents* can grow to seven feet tall, and require between eight to 12 years to fully mature.

Agave plants, unlike grape vines, cannot regrow. The plant is not reusable after harvest, so a new plant must be grown anew.

In Latin, *agave* translates as "illustrious", "admirable", and "noble". Damn right.

*Not cactus!

Nobody Expects the Spanish Inquisition!

When Cortes' Spaniards invaded the Aztec empire in 1519, it wasn't long before their booze supplies ran low.

So, they stood on the shoulders of the Aztecs and refined pulque into mezcal wine, using their crafty European distillation techniques.

Know Thy Tequila

It is the heart, the *piña*, of the

BLUE AGAVE PLANT

that is distilled to produce tequila.
The hearts, which usually
weigh approx. 30lbs, are cut out,
cooked / steamed, milled (ground down)
and then fermented.

Drinkers' Lingo

Tequila slammin' may seem as simple as one, two, three, floor, but if you want to drink the good stuff, try to remember these age and distillation terms and conditions:

Blanco

- Blanco, or silver, tequila is aged for two-months, often less.
- 100 per cent blue agave blanco tequila is considered the purest form of tequila.

Reposado

- Aged between two and 11 months.
- Reposado means "rest".

Añejo

- Aged between one to five years.*

*Extra Añejo: a minimum of three years

UNITED STATES OF TEQUILA

In 2019, the United States bought more than 240,000,000 bottles of tequila, approximately 80 per cent of the world's total supply.

The top five states that consume the most tequila are:

1. Nevada

2. Colorado

3. Arizona

4. California,

and (who would have guessed…)

5. Maryland

Straight and Neat

Dame un tequila derecho, por favor

Sip, swirl and savour your tequila. When
in Rome (or Mexico), order your tequila the
traditional way – "*tequila derecho*".

Neat

If you wish, you can add a slice of lemon
and ice, though room temperature is
preferred for 100 per cent blue agave
premium tequilas.

Tequilatails:

LA PALOMA

Just because Jimmy Buffett built his house in Margaritaville doesn't mean to say it's everyone's home. La Paloma is the undisputed, if often underrated, tequila cocktail champion.

Mix and Match:

1½ oz tequila

4 oz grapefruit soda, or juice

Juice of half a lime

Pinch of salt

Lime wheel and sprig of mint, to garnish

Make It Right:
- Two large cubes of ice.
- Tequila.
- Add the salt.
- Squeeze the lime half into the glass and then drop into the glass.
- Fill the glass up with grapefruit soda.
- *Ariba!*

Pulque Fiction

A thousand years ago, the Aztecs squeezed out the agave plant sap and fermented it, creating a drink known as *pulque*. If done right,

98 PER CENT

of the juice from the *piña* can be extracted.

Potted History: Agave Plant

The term mezcal refers to agave spirits
that derive from the agave plant.

But ONLY tequila comes from the

BLUE AGAVE SPECIES.

So, tequila is a mezcal – but not all
mezcals are tequila. Got it?

Bottles Up!

No two tequila bottles are alike. They now come in all shapes, sizes and sophistication.

The daddy, or *padre*, of tequila bottles is the Don Julio bottle – more than 80 per cent of all tequila brands use this iconic squat shape, including Patrón. Before it was invented in the 1960s, and used by the Don Julio brand, tequila bottles looked like elongated wine bottles, blown by local glassmakers to represent the tall, sharp shape of an agave plant leaf.

However, these tall bottles would obstruct guests' faces when left on the table at dinner parties. Don Julio Gonzalez wanted something different for his brand. He commissioned glassblowers to make a short, fat bottle with a wood cap, a bottle that could be seen, and kept, on the table every time he threw a party. Marketing genius.

Five Mezcals Not to Forget

There are now more than 250 recorded agave plant species. Tequila comes from just one – the blue agave. However, other spirts can also be made from other species. Work up a thirst and hunt these other mezcal-esques down too…

Mezcal

The *espadin* species of the agave plant is used, predominantly, to make mezcal. Though around 30 species of agave also do the same trick. Tequila is typically produced by steaming the agave hearts. Mezcal, however, is roasted.

Bacanora

This mezcal Bacanora comes from Sonora, the Mexican state that runs parallel to the Gulf of California and shares a border with Arizona. Distillation of Bacanora was illegal until 1992. Sonora translates as "pleasant sounding"; Bacanora translates to "pleasant drinking" (maybe).

Raicilla

Raicilla comes from the same state as tequila, Jalisco, but more towards Puerto Vallarta. Locals called it "little root", or Raicilla, and it has been considered moonshine until just recently.

Pulque

Pulque is, in essence, an alcoholic milkshake. It is made from the fermented sap from all species of the agave plant. Pulque was the first alcoholic drink enjoyed by the Aztecs and was stolen by the Spanish and distilled into modern tequila when they invaded Montezuma's Aztec empire.

Sotol

Hailing from the Chihuahua region of northern Mexico, Sotol is made in the same way as mezcal and tequila, but it uses another succulent plant, the Dasylirion, not the agave.

CHAPTER
TWO

HECHO EN MEXICO

Know Thy Tequila

We doubt this needs saying, but once you open your tequila bottle, it's best to drink it all within

TWO MONTHS.

Don't leave it in the cupboard between Christmases.

Unlike whiskey, or scotch, or gin, oxidation and evaporation lowers the quality of tequila and destroys the agave profile.

After six months, any leftover tequila will start tasting more like bourbon.

Know Thy Tequila

Blanco tequila is considered the "healthiest" tequila.

It includes agavin, which lowers blood sugar levels, and inulin, which aids in the digestion of food.

Tequila Cocktail:

BARACK OBAMA'S MARGARITA

Former US president Barack Obama's favourite cocktail is a classic margarita.

Here's his recipe:

Mix and Match:

3 oz tequila, preferably reposado 100 per cent agave tequila

½ cup cointreau

1 cup fresh lime juice, plus a little extra for moistening the rim of the glasses

A pinch of sugar (if required)

Kosher salt, for crusting the rim of the glasses

Three cubes of medium-sized ice

Make It Right:

- In a small jug, toss in the tequila, orange liqueur and lime.
- Taste.
- Add a bit more lime or a pinch of sugar, if necessary.
- Moisten the rim of glasses with lime juice and dip in salt.
- Pour half of the margarita mixture into a cocktail shaker, add half of the ice cubes.
- Shake for 15 seconds.
- Strain into the glasses, then add the remaining margarita mixture.

Hit or Myth

A long-held tequila myth is that it gives you hangovers worse than any other spirit or alcoholic drink. This isn't true.

Any "real" tequila that is made with 100 per cent pure blue agave will not include the sugars, corn syrups and congeners that 51 per cent "mixto" tequilas have, and thus will not inflict a hangover on your poor brain.

Until the year 2000,

98 PER CENT

of all tequilas imbibed in the US were mixto tequilas.

40

66

It would be very
strange to see Keith
Richards in top form
without the company
of a good tequila."

99

*Peter Rudge, the Rolling Stones tour promoter, in notes sent
to venues ahead of a band's show, 1973*

In the Limelight:

TEREMANA *NOM: 1613*

While owner and founder Dwayne Johnson may be a big Hollywood superstar with huge thighs, his tequila brand is all about small-batch, hand-crafted, 100 per cent blue agave. And, like Dwayne Johnson in most of his films, Teremana is all about saving the world too – it's one of the most sustainable and environmentally friendly brands on the market.

Produced from the highlands of Jalisco, the name Teremana comes from TERA, of the earth, and MANA, a powerful Polynesian spirit that guides the company's success. Apparently.

CANTARITOS POT

If you find yourself lost in Tequila, find yourself a clay pot, called a *cantarito*, and fill it with tequila, lime and grapefruit soda.

This traditional cocktail is popular in Tequila and the pots themselves make a great souvenir to remember your trip, just in case the tequila makes your memory fuzzy.

A Little Horse, Part 2

These little *caballito's* have a history too, as legend would tell it...

Jimadors, the agave farmers who cut down the agave plant, travelled between fields on horseback. Swinging by their saddles were gourds filled with water. One day, a farmer asked one of his jimadors why he hung two gourds from his saddle – one filled with water and the other with tequila. The gourd filled with tequila had a bull's horn alongside it. "One gourd is mine," said the jimador, the other is – *para my caballito* – "for my horse". Soon, farmers all around Jalisco began calling the last shot of tequila, "one for my *caballito*", and the bull's horn used to slam tequila back was given the name, *el caballito* and, well, the rest is drunk history.

❝

A little tequila,
sunshine
and tacos never hurt
anybody.

❞

Ron Woodroof (played by Matthew McConaughey),
Dallas Buyers Club, 2013.

As seen on IMDB.com

Tequila Fact

In 1964, automobile manufacturer Chrysler developed an engine that would run on anything flammable, including tequila.

They built three prototypes (Jay Leno owns one). They never went into production due to their expense – about $400,000 in today's money (the equivalent of ten Tesla Model 3s!).

Tequila Fact

Before the 1800s, tequila (as we know it today) didn't exist. It was called "mezcal wine".

It wasn't until 1873 that mezcal wine from Tequila, Jalisco, officially became called tequila, to distinguish itself from the mezcal produced in the south of Mexico.

HIGH AND LOW

Like all fine French wine and fizz, tequila is the product of its *terroir* – a word that brings together all of the surrounding environmental aspects that help the agave plant to flourish: geography, water, soil, weather, sunlight.

Tequilas made in the Highlands (Los Altos) of Jalisco have sweeter, more floral, delicate flavour profiles. Those made in the Lowland (El Valle) are enriched by volcanic soil and taste spicier, earthier and more mineral.

Tequila in a Barrel

For the ageing of Añejo and Extra Añejo tequila, American and French oak barrels – that once held bourbon, cognac or wine – are used.

These barrels impart unique flavours to the tequila, as per the brand's master distiller's own request. Bourbon barrels are the most predominant.

Serving Suggestion

Tequila is best stored at
room temperature and savoured
the same way.

For tequila-based cocktails,
put your glass (and lemon wedge)
in the freezer for 20 minutes
ahead of schedule.

This will cool down your cocktail
mixers so that your drink is not
just one big lukewarm mess.

UNITED STATES OF TEQUILA

With more than 45 million regular tequila drinkers – roughly the population of California – the US consumes twice as much tequila as Mexico.

The state that drinks the most tequila? California. Coincidence?

Hit or Myth

If you've ever felt proud that you once drunk tequila with a worm in the bottle, chances are you're just another sucker of a marketing campaign. However, the "tequila worm" myth is rooted in some medicinal purpose, traced back to the 1940s.

As tequila/mezcal production took off, manufacturers would test the purity of their beverage by dropping a gusano, a type of caterpillar that fed on agave plants (not a worm), into the tequila. If the "worm" remained in one piece, the percentage of alcohol was high enough to pickle it.

> **"**
> Don't let it end
> like this.
> Tell them, I said
> something.
> **"**

Pancho Villa's final words.

The infamous Mexican revolutionary, an icon of tequila, the Hispanic Robin Hood, infamously didn't drink tequila, or any alcohol at all, for that matter. This is why a tequila cruda was often called "Pancho Villa style", I guess because he was a fast shooter?

Tequila Fact

In 2005, J. B. Wagoner, a Californian tequila lover, made a spirit from the blue agave that grew on his property in Temecula. (Blue agave can grow in some southern US states.)

He called it Temequila. He immediately received a "stop it" letter from the Tequila Regulatory Council, who demanded he change the name. The word tequila is fiercely protected by the TRC.

Tequila Fact

The tequila you drink today was made from a seed that was planted ten years ago. So, when tequila sales increased dramatically in the US in the 2000s, agave farmers were shocked – the supply could not meet demand, and agave prices rose by

900 PER CENT!

Now, more than 50 million agave plants are harvested every year – one tenth of all the blue agave plants currently maturing (500 million).

Know Thy Tequila

Tequila is harvested by hand by farmers known as *jimadors*. They chop the 200 or so spikey agave leaves off the plant using a large blade known as a *coa*.

Jimadors require years of experience to be able to identify a ripe agave, as well as physical strength: experienced jimadors can harvest more than 100 agave hearts every day.*

*In 2019, 50 million agave plants were harvested in total.

Never confuse mezcal with mescaline.
They are not the same.

MEZCAL

is a spirit distilled from the agave plant; *mescaline* is a hallucinogenic seed found in the peyote cactus.

Now you know.

TASTE THY TEQUILA

Tequila, in every way, is like a fine wine. And should be treated, and tasted, accordingly. Here's how to scratch and sniff tequila the Mexican way… in your home.

1. Grab a champagne flute, or normal wine glass.

2. Pour approx. 1½ oz of your favourite premium tequila (a single shot) into it.

3. Swirl the tequila gently around the glass. Observe the "legs" that appear on the glass as you swirl. Rule of thumb: The longer it takes these legs to reach the bottom of the glass, the better the tequila.

4. Swirl the spirit again, but this time tilt the glass to the point where the tequila is almost spilling out. While tilting, observe (with your nose) the tequila's aroma at the bottom, middle and top of the glass. The heavier aromas will settle at the bottom while the lighter ones will float to the top.

5. Sip. But don't swallow. Allow the tequila to caress your tongue. Smell the tequila again, as your mouth bonds with the spirit. Swallow with style.

6. Sip again. This time with pursed lips and intake with a slow breath. Savour all the flavour profiles and aromas you can. Write them down, if you must.

7. Do this on repeat until you love your family once again.

Tequila Distilleries: Top Ten

There are currently 135 active tequila distilleries
operating in Mexico. These distilleries make all the
tequila for the 900 or so tequila companies, and
more than 2,000 individual brand names. These are
distilleries, considered doing God's work:

1. **NOM 1579** (El Pandillo)
2. **NOM 1493** (Tequila Los Abuelos)
3. **NOM 1108** (Jorge Salles Cuervo y Sucesores,
       S.A. de C.V.)
4. **NOM 1120** (Tequila Siete Leguas)
5. **NOM 1518** (Tequila Casa de Los Gonzalez)
6. **NOM 1123** (Tequila Cascahuín, S.A.)
7. **NOM 1468** (Grupo Tequilero Mexico,
       S.A. de C.V.)
8. **NOM 1139/1474** (Tequila Tapatio (La Alteña))
9. **NOM 1508** (Fabrica de Tequila Don Nacho,
       S.A. de C.V.)
10. **NOM 1560** (Tequilas Gonzalez Lara, S.A. de C.V.
       (Casa Marengo)

Know Thy Tequila

Premium sipping tequilas, such as Patrón, employ the traditional "Tahona" process in order to crush the steamed agave hearts.

This process involves taking a donkey, or mule, for a short circular walk while dragging a two-ton volcanic stone wheel over the cooked agave *piñas*.

The resulting juice and fibres squashed out of the agave are then placed in pine wood casks for fermentation. The juice is then fine filtered and double distilled into, finally, tequila.

Dial M for

MARGARITA

Margarita is Spanish for daisy – not
Margaret. Duh! And the margarita cocktail
is derived from the iconic and historic
Tequila Daisy cocktail. Make it…

Mix and Match:

½ oz fresh lemon juice
½ tsp fine sugar
3 oz tequila (double
    shot)

½ ounce Grand Marnier
Ice
Club soda, to top

Make It Right:

- In a shaker, mix the lemon juice and sugar.
- Throw in the tequila and Grand Marnier.
- Stack the glass with ice.
- Give it a shake and strain into a chilled glass of
  your choice.
- Top off with soda.

66

A tequila drink without a lot of mess in it.

99

*Jazz singer Peggy Lee, asking for a tequila drink in the 1940s.
And by doing so, perhaps inventing the fuss-less margarita.*

Sales of Tequila boomed
during the COVID-19
lockdown of summer 2020
with an increase of

64.3 PER CENT

over a three-month period.

Cognac, which saw sales rise
by 67 per cent, was the only
spirit to see more sales.

Tequila History

After each agave plant is harvested, every part of the plant can be re-used.

The *piñas* make tequila.

The 200 or so leaves of the plant, with their super-strong fibres, are cut off and are ideal for producing mats, ropes and cloths.

Even wigs!

In 2019, tequila sales generated more than 40 billion Mexican pesos (MXN). That's

FOUR MILLION TIMES

more than the average Mexican worker's annual salary (100 MXN).

Tequila Fact

Despite many premium tequilas nipping at its tipsy heels, José Cuervo is still the leading tequila brand in the United States, with more than 3.87 million 9-litre cases sold in 2019.

It is also the best-selling tequila in the world, with a more than 35 per cent market share of the tequila sector globally.

Yep, one in three shots is a José!

Potted History: Agave

While many variants of the 200 agave plants
are native to several Mexican states, and
southern US states, the blue agave is native
only to the Mexican states of Jalisco, Colima,
Nayarit and Aguascalientes. The plant prefers
above-sea-level altitudes of more than
1,500 metres (5,000 feet).

In the Limelight:

JOSÉ'S HOUSE NOM: 1122

In 1758, Ferdinand VI, the king of Spain, granted permission to Don José Antonio de Cuervo to cultivate and harvest the blue agave plant in Jalisco. In 1795, the first "Vino Mezcal de Tequila de José Cuervo" was made.

This was the start of the tequila industry. Their Cuervo distillery, La Rojeña, is in the centre of Tequila, the town, and was officially founded in 1812.

UNITED STATES OF TEQUILA

In the US, in 2019, three major tequila brands generated more than half of the country's total tequila volume sales.

Can you guess the brands?*

*(Cuervo, Patrón and Sauza.)

Tequila Fact

While 350 million litres of tequila
were sold in 2019, whisky sold more
than 3.5 billion.

Tequila represents just 1 per cent
of the global spirits market, and just
7 per cent of the US spirit market.

But for how much longer?

CHAPTER
THREE

NO WAY JOSÉ

Know Thy Tequila

Renowned artist, and First Lady of Mexico, Frida Kahlo was said to have drank a bottle of tequila every day in order to merely survive the demons that tormented her. Her dependency gave rise to two of her most powerful quotes:

"I tried to drown my sorrows, but the bastards learned how to swim."

"Doctor, if you let me drink this tequila, I promise I won't drink at my funeral."

Frida Kahlo

66

Life is like a
bad margarita with
good tequila.

99

Peter Applebome, 1985. As seen in the LA Times, 1985

"

A computer lets you
make more mistakes faster
than any invention in
human history, with the
possible exception
of handguns and tequila.

"

Mitch Ratcliffe, 1992

Tequilalogy

65 per cent of
UK drinkers prefer to
drink tequila
in cocktails rather than
as a shot.

MIX YOUR DRINKS

100 per cent blue agave tequila needs no mixer – it's that smooth – but if you want to pace yourself, these are the most complementary mixers.

1. **Sparkling, or soda water**
   (Add a citrus wheel, of course)

2. **Pineapple juice**
   Turn your tequila tropical with pineapple juice. Dilute it down, if using it straight from a can, so as to not completely lose the tequila taste.

3. Orange juice
Whisk orange juice into your tequila to give your breakfast more of a party vibe!

4. Agave syrup / honey
Mix some sweet clear honey or agave syrup into sparkling soda water and a shot of tequila – sweet and sour at the same time.

5. Vermouth
Because everything tastes better with vermouth!

6. Milk
Nah, just kidding.

66

I've been all over
the world drinking
tequila.
You can't have a party
without tequila.

99

Oprah Winfrey. As seen on YouTube, 8 November 2017

Tequila Measure

It takes

10 LITRES OF WATER

to produce

1 LITRE OF TEQUILA.

Tequila Cocktail:

TEQUILA OIL

Named in honour of Mexico's petrol boom in the late 1970s, the Tequila Oil cocktail is deceptively seductive – and simple to make.

Pour a double serving of your favourite tequila. Mix in a large tablespoon of tomato juice.

Now, here's the kickers – add habanero chilli sauce and a spoonful of HP "brown" sauce. Mix.

It'll look like oil – and it'll grease your wheels for the whole day.

Tequilalogy

In the US,
mezcal sales have
grown

279 PER CENT

since 2010.

"

A shot of that
Mexican drink that
they call – no,
I've forgotten the
name, but it lifts
the top of your
head off.

"

P. G. Wodehouse, Jeeves Takes Charge, *1916*

66

We should all
believe in something,
and I believe
it's time
for another shot
of tequila.

99

Justin Timberlake, on Twitter, 1 September 2012

UNITED STATES OF TEQUILA

In the US, the average
tequila consumer skews slightly
younger − 37.8 years of age, on
average, compared to an average
age of 38.7 for overall liquor sales.

Also, 50.91 per cent of
tequila purchasers are men and
49.09 per cent are women.

Know Thy Tequila

The US hogs all the world's tequila, guzzling down 204 million litres of the stuff a year. But the rest of the world is getting wise too.

Here are the other top ten tequilaholics:

- **Germany** – 5 million litres (40 times fewer than the US!)
- **Spain** – 3.7 million litres
- **France** – 3.5 million litres
- **Japan** – 2.3 million litres
- **Canada** – 2 million litres
- **UK** – 2 million litres
- **Latvia** – 1.7 million litres
- **Italy** – 1.6 million litres
- **Colombia** – 1.4 million litres
- **South Africa** – 1.3 million litres

Know Thy Tequila

According to the *Cheers On-Premise Handbook*, in 2008 Americans consumed more than 185,000 margaritas per hour on average.

In 2010, the margarita was the most popularly ordered drink at bars in 2010, representing 18 per cent of all mixed-drink sales in the US.

Know Thy Tequila

According to the Mexican Agriculture Ministry, in 2020, the tequila industry generates more than

70,000 JOBS

and represents Mexico's fifth largest agricultural export, after beer, avocados, tomatoes and berries.

Tequila Playlist

The most famous song about tequila is, without a doubt, The Champs' "Tequila", written by Danny Flores.

It was a US No. 1 hit on 28 March 1958 on both the pop and R&B charts and is identifiable by, of course, its mambo beat and that famous dirty sax solo. You know the one. Da-na-na-na-na-na-na – Tequila!

Tequila Playlist

The tequila shots might be good – but these hits differ greatly in quality.

- **"Tequila Sunrise"** – The Eagles
- **"Tequila"** – Terrorvision
- **"Tequila"** – The Champs
- **"Tequila Makes Her Clothes Fall Off"** – Joe Nichols
- **"Margaritaville"** – Jimmy Buffett
- **"On the Tequila"** – Alanis Morissette
- **"Hot Tequila Brown"** – Jamiroquai
- **"Tequila Sheila"** – Bobby Bare
- **"Tequila Talkin"** – Lonestar
- **"Ten Rounds with José Cuervo"** – Tracy Byrd

Tequilalogy

Without a doubt the greatest sketch
about tequila ever committed to celluloid.
Yes, it's *The Three Amigos*.

Bartender: "We don't have no beer. Just tequila."
Ned Nederlander: "What's tequila?"
Bartender: "It's like beer."
Dusty Bottom: "Is it fattening?"
Bartender: "Fattenings?"
Lucky Day: "Forget it. If it's like beer, we'll have
    some. Three tequilas."
Bartender: "Sure. Sure, amigos. Enjoy yourselves.
    But try not to get into too much trouble, okay?"
    *[The Amigos drink tequila and their bodies jolt
    dramatically to it]*
Ned Nederlander: "It's an odd taste, isn't it?"
Lucky Day: *[high pitch voice]* "It's probably
    watered down."

The Three Amigos, 1986

Tequila Takes Time

Vines mature their grapes after 365 days. Tequila's blue agave take approx.

3,000 DAYS TO MATURE

before they are harvested. And then the plant is never reused again.

Remember, tequila takes time. So, take your time with tequila.

Know Thy Tequila

In 1532, the recent invaded throngs of Spanish"discovered" the state of Jalisco. Upon "arrival" they met a tribe of natives known as the "Tiquili", a faction of the Toltecs.

Their village was called "Tequitlan" – or the "land of hard labour". It was later shortened by the Spaniards to "Tequila".

Approximately 45 per cent
of all tequila is produced around
the town of

❝

Tequila. Straight.
There's a real polite drink.
You keep drinking until
you finally take one more
and it just won't go down.
Then you know you've
reached your limit.

❞

American actor Lee Marvin, a legendary tequila enthusiast.
As seen on DNA India.com, October 2011

Margaritaville

Tequila's greatest fan, Jimmy Buffett, released his first (and only) Top 10 single, "Margaritaville".

The tune describes the singer's love of Margarita – "a Mexican cutie" – and the laidback island-living lifestyle.

It was Jimmy to which the famous / atrocious margarita quote is attributed – "If life gives you limes, make margaritas" – as well as the reputation of tequila as a party spirit.

Know Thy Tequila

Want to know how much agave makes one bottle of tequila?

Remember the seven-to-one weight-to-volume ratio rule? A single agave *piña* that weighs approx. 30lbs / 14kgs will produce roughly 12 pints / 6 litres of tequila, or eight 25oz / 750ml bottles.

Know Thy Tequila

In 2005, it was estimated that 70 per cent of all tequila consumed in the USA was used for margaritas.

In 2020, 50 per cent of all tequila consumed in the US is sipping tequila.

Know Thy Tequila

Agave is ready for harvest once the *piña* (the central bulb) has reached a sugar content of approximately 24 per cent and is large enough to produce sufficient quantities of juice.

Harvest usually occurs in the dry season when sugar content is much higher than the water-logged wet season.

All the leaves are then removed and a sharp stake is driven through the base of the plant to cut off the roots and allow the whole *piña* to be taken away for processing.

The town of

TEQUILA

was officially established in

1666

Know Thy Tequila

There are currently 500,000,000 agave plants in Mexico across more than 125,000 hectares, and 25,000 agave plantations. Large-scale producers harvest approximately 325,000 agave plants each per year. Around 50 million agave are harvested every year.

Know Thy Tequila

The José Cuervo brand was quick to capitalize on the increasing popularity of the margarita cocktail by launching its first-ever US ad campaign in 1945 with the slogan

"Margarita: It's more than a girl's name".

It would become America's most popular cocktail and it is estimated that about 60 per cent of all tequila sold in the US goes into margaritas.

MIXTOS

The mid-twentieth-century downfall of tequila started in 1970, when tequila producers asked the Mexican government for permission to dilute tequila with other cane sugars as the demand for tequila increased, but agave crops simply could not meet the demand.

The government said yes, giving rise to the 51 per cent agave "mixtos". These mixtos would come to define tequila in the US, and the world, for the next few decades and give tequila the bad reputation it never deserved.

Know Thy Tequila

Tequila bottles are now as iconic as the spirit they contain. But for the first 200 years of tequila's commercial production, tequila would predominantly be sold in demijhon containers – 3- to 10-gallon bulbous narrow-necked bottles, enclosed in wicker covers.

In 1903, with the invention of the world's first completely automatic glass-forming machine – a machine for making bottles – tequila could suddenly be squeezed into a bottle and mass produced.

Know Thy Tequila

At the start of World War II,
tequila exports in
the US boomed from 21,000
litres in 1941 to

4,500,000

by 1946, due to the
destruction or closure of
90 per cent of Europe's wine
and spirit distilleries.

Know Thy Tequila

Bourbon is the national spirit of the US.

Gin is the UK's national spirit.

Tequila is Mexico's national spirit.

World's Best Tequila

According to the experts at the
annual World Tequila Awards, the
best tequila on planet earth is
– drum roll –

CIERTO TEQUILA'S RESERVE COLLECTION EXTRA AÑEJO.

The tequila is made at the legendary
La Tequileña distillery (NOM 1146),
located in the heart of the town
of Tequila.

108

In the Limelight:

TRES COMAS TEQUILA

Tres Comas Tequila, the fictional tequila brand from the hit HBO TV show *Silicon Valley*, is now available to buy. The brand, created by fictional (and obnoxious) billionaire Russ Hanneman (portrayed by Chris Diamantopoulos), is said to be the only tequila acceptable for billionaires. The character was clearly a dig at celebrity-endorsed, and -owned, tequila brands.

While the tequila's creator may be fictional, the brand has very much come to life. It is now made by Diageo (NOM 1535).

"Tres Comas is literally the best tequila on the market. I drink it, so that's how you know."

Tesla Tequila

In November 2020, Elon Musk entered the tequila business with his own super-premium brand of tequila – Tesla Tequila!

The instantly-iconic bottle, shaped like a lightning bolt, contains tequila made from sustainably sourced highland and lowland agaves and was aged for 15 months in French oak barrels. Tasters lucky enough to get their hands on the bottle report the spirit has notes of fruit, vanilla, cinnamon and pepper.

Tesla Tequila started off as an April Fool's Day prank in 2018 when Musk promoted the spirit with an Instagram post that read, "Coming soon to Tesla merch. Teslaquila. Free shots in stores every April 1st."

The joke soon became real. Before it even been released, every $250 bottle of Tesla Tequila had sold out.

What on earth (or on mars) will Musk do next?

Know Thy Tequila

A recent study by Patrón to celebrate the US's National Tequila Day (24 July) has shown that 65 per cent of drinkers choose to drink tequila in cocktails rather than as a shot.

The same poll showed that only 23 per cent of drinkers know that tequila is distilled from agave; 77% of those polled thought it was made with other sources such as grain, botanicals, potatoes or lime. Oops.

Little Miss Tequila

The baby name Tequila has been given to girls in the United States (mainly in Texas and California) ever since 1958, with more than 2,154 girls given the name. Tequila gained the most popularity as a name in 1989, when its usage went up by 193.41 per cent.

Strangely enough, 1989 was also the year Patrón was introduced to the world as the first premium tequila. So, the name was at least classy back then.

During that year, 127 babies were named Tequila, according to BabyCenter.com.

66

Tequila!
From darkness, there
is light!

99

Steve Hadley (played by Bradley Whitford),
The Cabin in the Woods, *2011*

IP TEQUILA

In 1974, as the world watched the Watergate scandal unfold, the Mexican government quietly claimed the word "Tequila" as its intellectual property while no one was looking. This proved to be a huge marketing win. The government secured a denomination of origin (AOC), meaning tequila can only be produced in Mexico.

Today, no other product on earth can be called tequila, nor can tequila be made or sold anywhere else but Mexico. A few years later, the Tequila Regulatory Council was created to promote the culture surrounding tequila, as well as ensure the quality of each distillery.

"

I believe — to the best of my recollection, anyway — that I soon made the classic error of moving from margaritas to actual shots of straight tequila. It does make it easier to meet new people.

"

Chef Anthony Bourdain. As seen on FirstWeFeast.com, 24 July 2016

CHAPTER
FOUR

WORTH A SHOT

Would a Rose by Any Other Name?

The word "tequila" has a mysterious etymology. Some believe the word comes from a Mexican tribe, the Nahuatl, with the words "tequitl" and "tlan" translated as "place of work".

Others believe "tequila" is a corruption of the word "tetilla", or "small breast", which has historically been the name for the conical-shaped summit of the strato volcano near Tequila, whose eruption 200,000 years ago enriched the land with fertile soils to grow the agave species.

66

We very much wanted to talk
to the ladies, but we often
didn't have the nerve, so we'd
drink a couple of shots of
tequila and suddenly it was,
'Howdy, ma'am.'

99

*Glenn Frey, of the Eagles, discussing tequila
and the band's hit song "Tequila Sunrise"*

❝

It's true
what they say,
you don't buy tequila,
you rent it.

❞

Karen Walker (played by Megan Mullally),
Will & Grace, Season 7, Episode 2, 2005

66

Oh boy, oh boy, oh boy,
oh boy, oh boy.

99

*Tess McGill (played by Melanie Griffith), after drinking
a few tequila shots,* Working Girl, *1988*

THE TEQUILA TOAST

There may be three ways to drink tequila (slam, sip and mix), but the traditional tequila toast is always the same no matter where you are.

¡Arriba! ¡Abajo!
¡Al centro! ¡Y Pa'dentro!

Glasses up! Glasses down!
Glasses to the front! Drink!

"

What kind of a diet doesn't allow tequila?

"

Owen Grady (played by Chris Pratt), Jurassic World, 2015

Know Thy Tequila

Tequila is good for your bones.

In a study in 2016, mice who ingested fructans, compounds derived from the blue agave plant, produced nearly 50 per cent more osteocalcin.

This revelation has excited scientists, who think that the blue agave plant is the key to helping more than 200 million osteoporosis sufferers worldwide.

66

If the glass
is half-empty, add
tequila.

99

Pilgrim Rick, This Is Us, *season 1, Episode 8*

Tequila Cocktail:

TEQUILA SUNRISE

Name-checked in the famous Eagles song from the album *Hotel California* (and not the Mel Gibson film of the same name), Tequila Sunrises are the perfect cocktail to ensure you're still awake at dawn.

Mix and Match:
2 tsp grenadine
1½ oz tequila
1 tbsp triple sec
1 large orange, juiced
Juice of ½ lemon
1 cocktail cherry
Ice

Make It Right:

- Pour the grenadine into the base of a highball glass.

- Fill a cocktail shaker with ice and add the tequila, triple sec and fruit juices.

- Shake well.

- Add ice cubes to the highball glass then carefully strain the cocktail into it.

- Try not to disturb the grenadine.

- Garnish with the cherry.

Tequila Cocktail:

DIABLO ROJO

The Diablo Roja (Red Devil), also known as
El Diablo (The Devil), is the best way to get
tipsy on tequila since, well, every
other way.

Mix and Match:

1½ oz tequila blanco
½ oz lime juice
½ oz sugar syrup
2½ oz ginger beer
Ice

1–2 tsp crème de
 cassis, to finish
1 tsp pomegranate seeds
 (to garnish)

Make It Right:

- Half-fill a highball glass with ice.
- Add the tequila, lime and sugar syrup.
- Stir.
- Now top up with ginger beer.
- Stir again.
- Pour in the crème de cassis.
- Garnish with pomegranate seeds.
- Easy-peasy-no-tequila-queasy!

Tequila Cocktail:

TEQUINI

Tequini + martini = Tequini!

Mix and Match:
2½ oz tequila blanco
½ oz dry vermouth
Dash of Angostura
   bitters

Garnish: olive (or lemon
   twist)

Make It Right:
- Place your glass in your freezer for 20 minutes before serving.
- Pour the tequila, dry vermouth and Angostura bitters into a cocktail shaker filled with ice.
- Shake.
- Strain.
- Plop in an olive.
- Enjoy!

66

I enjoy tequila
– it makes parties
more fun than warm
white wine.

99

Simon Sebag Montefiore. As seen on
Standard.co.uk, 15 June 2017

Oranges and Lemons

If you must insist on shooting tequila, may we recommend replacing the line of salt with brown sugar, and switching out the lemon wedge with an orange one.

And using

100 PER CENT AGAVE

– none of that mixto nonsense.

It's slightly more…classy.

Tequila by the Numbers

In 2020, in the United States alone, tequila has generated more than

$1.25 BILLION

in sales year-to-date as of 25 July 2020.

TEQUILA CRUDA

Salt. Tequila. Lemon. Job done.

Tequila cruda, or tequila shots, dates back to the 1930s, after the Spanish Influenza epidemic struck down one-third of the world's entire population and killed approx. 50 million people, including

675,000 AMERICANS.

Doctors at the time prescribed the remedy of tequila with salt and lemon, believing they would aid the body absorb the tequila quicker.

66

I looked at Teremana
as an opportunity to create
a tequila experience that
brings people together
in good times, not-so-good
times and everything
in between.

99

Dwayne Johnson on his tequila brand, Teremana.
As seen on People.com, 23 September 2020

Tequila Cocktail:

TEQUILA SLAMMER

Not to be confused with a *tequila cruda*, a Tequila Slammer is a much more refined drink (relatively). The key to a proper Tequila Slammer* is to slam the glass down and gulp the effervescent fizz as quickly as possible so the explosion of bubbles in your mouth tickles all your senses.

Here's how to do it right:

- Pour a double serving of tequila in an tumbler.
- Add an equivalent amount of a fizzy soda of your choice – grapefruit or lemon/lime tastes best.
- Cover the glass with a coaster, or your hand, and SLAM the glass down on the table.
- This will activate the fizz.
- Now, drink!

*Also known as a Tequila Boom or Tequilazo.

66

I'll have some tequila
aside to give him a shot
afterwards… maybe I should
give him the tequila before
to relax him up?

99

Lewis Hamilton, F1 World Champion, on "negotiating"
his multi-million-dollar Mercedes contract, with
team boss Toto Wolff.

As seen on PlanetF1.com, August 2020

Crystal Clear

Tequila cristalino, or crystal tequila, is the latest tequila trend phenomenon that has assisted the spirit's huge increase in popularity in the US in the past five years. "Cristalinos", as they are known, are premium aged tequilas that have been charcoal-filtered to remove any caramel colour that had been added by the barrel during the ageing process.

Cristalinos look like blanco but taste like añejo!

Know Thy Tequila

According to our good friends at Guinness World Records, the most expensive bottle of tequila ever sold was the Platinum & White Gold Tequila bottle, produced by the brand Ley .925, to a private collector in Mexico, in July 2006. The cost?

$225,000 (£120,000)

The price tag is deserved, naturally. Inside the limited-edition bottle was 100 per cent blue agave tequila that had been aged for six years – so a very rare thing, indeed.

"

I'm always like,
'Nope,
I can never
drink tequila again,'
but…

"

Jennifer Lawrence, Interview *magazine,*
12 January 2015

66

The bottle. Now.

99

Walter White (played by Bryan Cranston),
Breaking Bad, Season 2, Episode 10*

*Fans of Breaking Bad will understand the importance
of tequila to the show.

CHAPTER
FIVE

AGAVE
MY HEART TO
TEQUILA

Tequila Brand Slogans:
Part One

No tequila brand, premium or otherwise, is exempt from having an inspirational (read: cheesy) brand slogan. Here are the very best of the very worst.

- **Teremena** – Tequila of the people
- **Patrón** – Simply perfect.
- **Avion** – Step out of your shell.
- **Herradura** – Never compromise.
- **El Jimador** – Live 100%.
- **Gran Centenario** – The calling.
- **Sauza** – Life is harsh. Your tequila shouldn't be.
- **Sauza Conmemorativo** – The smoother, oak-aged tequila.
- **Sauza 901** – No limes needed.
- **José Cuervo** – Have a story.
- **José Cuervo Silver** – So smooth, it shatters expectations.
- **José Cuervo Cinge** – Get stung.

Dollar Signs

In 2019, the US dollar
retail sales of tequila in the
United States passed, for
the first time in tequila's
history, the double-digit
billion benchmark
with

10.3 BILLION DOLLARS.

66

When you actually really think
about it, it's a sort of strange thing
to do, to walk down a red carpet
with a ridiculously over-the-top-gown.
So I do tend to look at it as a sort of
spectacle, and embrace it as that. I have
fun. I get ready, enjoy the dressing-up
part. And I do a shot of tequila and
then get in the car.

99

Actress Emily Blunt on her red-carpet ritual.
As seen on Telegraph.co.uk

"

Get going again with
tequila on the rocks*. If you
only drink that stuff, you
won't get a hangover in
the first place!

"

*Russell Crowe has a love of good tequila.
As seen on Mirror.co.uk, January 2013*

*Russell's tequila of choice? The best – Silver Patrón.

Mexico's Tequila Production

Tequila's home nation, Mexico, has kept up (just about) with the US', and a few other nations', thirst for tequila.

Since 1995, with 104.3 million litres, Mexico has more than tripled its tequila production in 25 years with a new record production of

351.7 MILLION LITRES

of tequila in 2019, worth more than 1.8 billion dollars.

Margaritaville

Neat sipping tequila should be served at room temperature. Margaritas, however, must be served at the same temperature as revenge: cold as ice.

For the best Margarita known to mankind, stick your cocktail glass in the freezer for 20 minutes before it's needed. The frosty glass will retain its cool, and it means you don't have to worry about melting ice diluting your tequila. You're welcome.

Mirren's Shot at Glory

At 2018's Academy Award ceremony, British acting legend Helen Mirren boosted the popularity of tequila even further in the US, and across the pond, when she made headlines by necking a shot on the Oscars red carpet.

"It was just given to me," she said. "A nice shot of tequila for the nerves!" The next year, Jimmy Kimmel's side-kick, Guillermo, copied the act and handed out shots of the world's hottest tequila to the world's hottest people.

It's now a new tradition.

Tequila Brand Slogans:
Part Two

Even more inspiring/aspiring/confusing tequila brand slogans for you to hang your sombrero on...

- **José Cuervo Especial** – It makes you electric.
- **Corazón de Agave** – The good stuff.
- **1800 Tequila** – Enough said.
- **1800 Reposado** – When you're ready for a smooth tequila.
- **Olmeca** – Switch on the night.
- **Éxodo** – What's your flavour?
- **Hornitos** – Purer than your intentions.
- **Cazadores** – Never forget where you come from.
- **Don Julio** – Taste the Mexico you don't know.
- **El Mayor** – A handmade legacy.
- **Corralejo** – The big tequila of Mexico.
- **Espólon** – Let's stir things up.
- **Casamigos** – Brought to you by those who drink it.
- **Talero** – Life tastes better naturally... So should your tequila.

VIVA LA REVOLUTION!

In mid-2019, American president Donald Trump imposed 5 per cent tariffs (rising to 25 per cent) on all Mexican goods, a punishment to the bordering nation for not agreeing to new US measures to remedy illegal immigration. This tariff would include the multi-billion-dollar values of tequila entering the US, and would accompany Trump's controversial border wall to cut off the US's geography from Mexico.

In an act of defiance, Americans have been showing support for Mexicans by drinking even more tequila. According to the *New York Times*: "Drinking tequila, is a way to signal dissent from the presidency of Donald Trump, who has made a border wall between the United States and Mexico a priority."

Top Ten Tequilas:
United States

In recent years, drinking tequila has become the most American thing you can do. So, let's raise a toast to the top 10 tequila brands in the United States.

- **Margaritaville**
- **Don Julio**
- **El Jimador**
- **Montezuma**
- **Juarez**
- **Familia Camarena**
- **1800 Tequila**
- **Sauza**
- **Patrón**
- **José Cuervo**

Tequila Cocktail:

THARRO NEGRO

One of Mexico's most historic holidays, Día de los Muertos (Day of the Dead) sees the celebration of the infamous tequila "cocktail" – the Charro Negro. While the drink is just basically a single/double serving of tequila with a Mexican cola mixer, the history of the Charro Negro refers to the traditional Mexican cowboy who dressed in black to mourn a loved one. Hence the name – Black Cowboy.

Mix and Match:

2 oz tequila

4 oz Coca-Cola (Mexican cola is best, obviously!)

Wedge/wheel/slice of lime

Two large cubes of ice

Make It Right:

- In a highball glass, clink-clunk two ice cubes.

- Throw in a lime slice.

- Add your tequila.

- Drown the tequila in cola.

- Listen to that glorious fizz.

Tip:
If you're feeling salty,
bury the rim of the
glass in salt.

Top Ten Tequilas:
Mexico

Just because the US drinks the most tequila, doesn't mean to say that Mexicans aren't far behind. Want to drink tequila like a Mexican? Drink these: the ten most popular tequilas in Mexico…

- **Patrón**
- **Chinaco**
- **Tequila 1800**
- **Tapatio**
- **Ocho**
- **El Jimador**
- **Don Julio**
- **Gran Centenario**
- **José Cuervo Tradicional**
- **Herradura**

One of Mexico, and the United States, most popular and revered premium (but affordable) tequilas is

1800 TEQUILA.

While the brand is owned by the Beckmann family (who also own José Cuervo), the name 1800 Tequila originates from the year that tequila was first aged in oak barrels.

Infuse Your Own Tequila

Don't waste your hard-earned money on store-bought fancy "flavour infused" tequilas. Do it yourself at home. Here's how:

1. Buy a bottle of 100 per cent agave blanco tequila (blanco is milder in flavour than more aged tequilas)

2. Buy a plain large litre/quart container with a sealable lid.

3. Fill the jar with a handful of your chosen botanical/fruit/spice/herb/chilli/vegetable.

4. Place the jar somewhere quiet and dark. Let it infuse for four hours.

5. Shake the container. Then, let it soak for three days (shaking every few hours).

6. Strain the liquid from the chosen fruit/spice/herb/chilli/vegetable.

7. Drink.

Tip: jalapenos add spice; blueberries add pepper notes; cinnamon adds warmth; pineapple adds tropical zest; broccoli tastes disgusting, etc.

Volcán de Tequila

As with everything in life, it is the miracle of Mother Nature that infuses our man-made spirits with excellence.

Tequila is no different. The ancient Volcán de Tequila, or Tequila Volcano, located to the east of the town, rises to a height of 2,920 meters (9,580 feet) above sea level.

With its iconic conical stratovolcano shape, this volcano defined the taste of tequila today when it last erupted 200,000 years ago, covering the landscape in lava and ash and creating a super fertile environment for growing agave – native only to Mexico.

MEXICAN SPANISH

Next time you find yourself in a saloon, impress your friends with these nifty nuggets of tequila-based conversation.

- *La hora de salir* – Time to go out
- *Copa* – Spirit and mixer
- *Llename* – Fill me up
- *Un chupito* – A shot
- *Ponme otro* – Another one please
- *¿Cuanto cuesta?* – How much?
- *Venga otro más* – Damn it, give me one more
- *Buenas noches* – Good night
- *Estoy bien crudo hoy* – I'm very hungover today
- *¿Dónde es la peda?* – Where is the party?

Top Tequila:
US Spirit Sales

The US spirits industry has plenty of reasons to toast itself silly with tequila – 2019 was the tenth straight year in a row sales of spirits increased. The industry is now worth a cool $90 billion – and rising. Naturally, tequila is the new kid on the block enjoying the biggest growth spurt.

Tequila is taking the most market share from vodka and gin than any other spirit, and now makes up 8.3 per cent of all spirit spending in the US.

- **Vodka – 74.15**
- **Whiskey – 69.29**
- **Rum – 24.13**
- **Tequila – 20.12**
- **Gin – 9.76**

(Sales are in million nine-litre cases.)

Out to Sea

Ernest Hemingway loved tequila. Especially when out fishing. The author called it his "steering liquor". Hemingway enjoyed tequila so much that on his fishing boat, he built a small bar atop the bridge to avoid having to go up and down a ladder in-between drinks. We can respect that.

Supply and Demand

The tequila industry requires approximately 50 million blue agave plants to be harvested every year in order to keep with the current demand for tequila.

In 2011, however, only 17.7 million blue agaves were planted, due to mature in 2020–21.

Hold on to your sombrero – there may be a shortfall of tequila!

> **❝**
>
> I love Patrón. I also love
> Don Julio 1942 as a nice sipping
> tequila. It's so yummy. It has a little
> sweetness to it, which I usually don't
> like. My [ex]fiancé Justin Theroux
> actually makes the perfect margarita
> with it, because there's no agave,
> no sugar, no mix. It's pure tequila,
> lime juice, a squinch* of Cointreau.
> It's delicious.
>
> **❞**

Jennifer Anniston. As seen on E-online.com

*A squeezy pinch, right?

On the Tequila Road

"Don't drink to get drunk, drink to enjoy life" –
so said the era-defining American beat novelist,
Jack Kerouac. The *On the Road* writer developed a
taste for tequila on one of his many adventures to
Mexico. Kerouac's love of consuming margaritas, his
favourite drink, consumed him so much that in the
male bathrooms of the White Horse Tavern, New
York – Kerouac's haunt – a sign above the urinals
read "Kerouac go home" – a last order from the bar
for the writer to put down his trademark tequila
cocktail and sober up.

Kerouac's recipe was consistent:

- 2 oz tequila
- 1 oz triple sec (or Cointreau)
- 1 oz lime juice
- Shake well and strain into a cocktail glass.

"

Motto for the day:
Stop trying to make
everyone happy.
You're not tequila.

"

Emmy Rossum, on Twitter, 29 August 2017

“

Nobody leaves my
tequila worm dangling
in the wind.

”

Zorro (as played by Antonio Banderas), Zorro, 1998

CHAPTER
SIX

JALISCO-GO-GO

Tequilatails:

VAMPIRO

Originating in the village of San Luis Soyatlán, in Jalisco, around 40 years ago, a Vampiro is a tequila-based Bloody Mary, or Bloody Maria, if you want to be culturally sensitive. Traditional drunk with a straw out of a clear plastic bag. Suck one dry, today!

Mix and Match:

1½ oz tequila
2½ oz tomato juice
1 oz orange juice
¼ oz lime juice
½ slice onion, finely
   chopped

1 tablespoon clear honey
Few slices of fresh red
   chilli
A splash of Worcestershire
   sauce
Salt

Make It Right:

• Shake and strain everything over ice into a highball glass (or plastic bag).

Dreaming of Jalisco

Like fine French wine
and fizz, in order for tequila to
be made and sold as tequila, it
can only be produced in five
states in Mexico: Guanajuato,
Michoacán, Nayarit,
Tamaulipas, and Jalisco.

The latter, Jalisco, is far and
away the largest producer
of this blue agave nectar.

"

My first racy scene was the standing in the doorway, totally naked... And I was petrified. I'd come to work that morning and I was shaking, so scared, like, 'I can't do this.' But then, a member of the crew brought a flask of tequila. It really helped stop my hands shaking, and gave me a boost of confidence. Acting 101: three shots of tequila, and you'll be fine.

"

Margot Robbie on her now-iconic nude scene in Martin Scorsese's The Wolf of Wall Street. *She drank three shots of tequila before filming*

"

Acting used to be how
I paid the rent, but I sold a
tequila company for a
billion fucking dollars. I don't
need money.

"

*George Clooney (after selling his Casamigos tequila brand
for one billion dollars in 2018).*

As seen on Vanityfair.com, 6 November 2017

66

To remove
blood stains from
your conscience,
try frozen
margaritas.

99

Comedian Demetri Martin, on Twitter, 5 July 2012

Tequilalogy

Be the
TEQUILA.

Not the lime.

Tequila Drinking Games:
Mexican Stand-Off

This is a traditional Mexican drinking game.
Here are the rules:

Players sit in a circle, each with a shot glass.
Player One fills all of the shot glasses with water,
except one, which has tequila in it. Player One
then commands the group to neck their drinks.

The players then have to guess who has the
tequila shot. If Player One is caught out, they
have to drink another shot.

Next, another player fills up everyone's glass,
and the game goes round until every player has
taken turns to fill up the glasses.

The player who doesn't get caught out
nominates someone to drink their tequila.

Tequila Drinking Games:
Mexican Bar Dice

Known as Mexico, or 21, this traditional Mexican drinking game is simple to play.

Firstly, pour a shot. Player One then grabs two dice and rolls. Add up the roll total. Then Player Two does the same.

The object of the game is for each player to roll a lower combined dice total than the previous roller. If Player Two does, move on to the next player. If they don't, they know what to do…

Tequila Jokes

Why did the Mexican take his wife to the top of a cliff?

Tequila

I heard a rumour that tequila can be drunk neat. But I took it with a pinch of salt.

"I've been on a tequila diet... And I've lost 4 days already."

How do you get a computer drunk?

A screenshot of Tequila

In the US, a rule for post-work drinking is, "One and done." For tequila lovers, it is "Juan and Don!"

What do you call a man with a shot of tequila on his head?

A taxi.

How does Harry Potter order tequila shots?

"Patrón us!"*

*For Potter nerds, yes, we know he actually says "Expecto patronum!"

Tequila Drinking Games:
Sombrero Dance

Think Musical Chairs, but with tequila...

Nominate a player to be in charge of the music. They must keep their eyes closed.

In your group of players, Player One wears a sombrero (although any hat will do) and dances while the music plays. To keep things traditional, mariachi music is best.

As the dancing continues, the sombrero is passed from the head of one player to another – the player with the hat gets to choose how long they wear the sombrero. When the music is stopped, whoever last had the sombrero must drink tequila.

Tequila Drinking Games:
Tequila Piñata

This traditional children's game works wonders with tequila – as long as the children are in bed.

Using string, hang a bottle of tequila from a tree, or the ceiling, or wherever you are. Blindfold Player One, and spin them round three times.

    With a stick, Player One has three chances to smack the *piñata*. If they hit it, they win. If they don't, they drink.

> **"**
>
> We usually have margaritas on Thursdays, but since it's Tuesday I'll make an exception.
>
> **"**

Chelsea Handler.

As seen on Bustle.com, February 2017

> ## It's 4:58 on Friday afternoon. Do you know where your margarita is?

Author Amy Neftzger.

As seen on Goodreads.com

Know Thy Tequila

A single serving of tequila has approximately 70 calories.

Whisky and gin have around 100 calories per single serving.

This difference is why you see a lot of claims that "tequila is the healthiest alcohol" in the world. But let's be honest, no one drinks just one tequila, do they?

A margarita cocktail has approx. 200 calories.

Hijuelos

While it is the male *jimadors* that have historically harvested the hearts of the blue agave plant, it was the women of Tequila who were responsible for cultivating the blue agave plants.

The *hijuelos*, or little children, are the seeds of the blue agave plant, and more than 50 million *hijuelos* must be planted each year in order to keep up with the world's tequila demand.

Margherita Monday

In 2020, the classic, iconic tequila cocktail, the margarita, was placed

SEVENTH

on *Drinks International*'s list of the world's bestselling cocktails. It is the only tequila cocktail to remain in the top ten.

Tequila Jokes

A man walks into a bar and orders a shot of tequila. He then looks into his pocket. He does this over and over again.

Finally, the bartender asks why he orders a shot of tequila and afterwards looks into his pocket.

The man responded, "I have a picture of my wife in there and when she starts to look good then I'll go home."

Tequila Cocktail:

COHEN'S RED NEEDLE

Singer-songwriter, and all-round American idol, Leonard Cohen's favourite cocktail was, of course, tequila-infused. It made his voice extra gravelly, no doubt. However, Cohen's tequila fun was his own infamous creation, the 'Red Needle.'

Into one tall glass, about half-full of crushed ice, pour and drop:

- 2 oz tequila
- 1 slice lemon
- Fill the glass to the top with cranberry juice.

66

Oh God, that's tequila. That's literally neat tequila. He's gone off the rails!

99

British comedian Jack Whitehall drinks superstar Harry Styles' tipple of choice, believing it to be wine, at the 2020 Brit Awards, London. It was straight Casamigos tequila – disguised in a wine glass! Classic Styles.

Sierra Sombrero

One of Europe's most common, and popular, tequila brands, Sierra, makes an aesthetic impact on supermarket shelves. You know it. The bottle wears a little plastic sombrero.

However, this little hat is more than a gimmick. Did you know that you can use the hat for pouring a near-perfect single shot of tequila?

You can also fill the brim with salt, in order to create a perfect salt-rim for your margarita (without making a mess), as well as use the high-pointed crown as a lemon / lime squeezer!

Sheeran's Shot

"Five shots of white tequila – not Patrón though – and one shot of passion-fruit juice, please. Put the tequila on ice, and then let it sit for a bit. And then pour it over ice into the juice, then shake it."

Musician Ed Sheeran's love of white (silver) tequila is legendary.

This was the singer's order at ABC Kitchen, New York; an insight into Ed's particular tequila recipe (given to him by Russell Crowe). The melted ice dilutes the tequila.

¡Ay Caramba!

Good 100 per cent tequila makes you feel happy. Bad 51 per cent tequila makes you go wild. Use this handy glossary of Spanish interjections to help you express how your tequila makes you feel.

- *Por Dios* – God help me
- *Buena suerte* – good luck
- *Huy* – ouch
- *Guay* – cool
- *Vale* – okay
- *Guau/Caramba* – wow
- *¡Arriba!* – hooray!
- *Bravo* – bravo
- *Gracias a Dios* – thank God
- *Qué horror* – how awful
- *Qué lástima* – what a shame
- *Ay de mí* – oh my
- *Ándale* – hurry up
- *Cuidado* – look out